iPad Mini User's Guide: Simple Tips and Tricks to Unleash the Power of your Tablet!

By Shelby Johnson

www.techmediasource.com

Disclaimer:

This eBook is an unofficial guide for the Apple iPad Mini and is not meant to replace any official documentation that came with the device. The information in this guide is meant as recommendations and suggestions, but the author bears no responsibility for any issues arising from improper use of the tablet. The owner of the device is responsible for taking all necessary precautions and measures with the tablet.

www.techmediasource.com

Author Introduction

Hello, I'm bestselling Kindle eBook author, Shelby Johnson. Among the previous titles I've released are *Facebook for Beginners: Navigating the Social Network* and *Kindle Fire HD User's Guide Book: Unleash the Power of Your Tablet!*, and *Kindle Paperwhite User Manual: Guide to Enjoying Your E-reader!*

I am a longtime technology enthusiast, and have also worked in the technology field. My previous work included helping seniors at a care center to learn to use the Internet and email basics. I've also worked as an IT project manager, helping to train employees on the use of various computer hardware and software. In case you're wondering, I also own an iPad Mini along with a Kindle Fire HD and the Kindle Paperwhite eReader, and I love all the devices for reading and other functions, but for tablet users, the iPad Mini often comes out on top as the best device to buy. I am not a salesperson, and I am not looking to give you a sales pitch for the item inside this eBook.

In this new iPad Mini User Manual, it is my goal to help others to understand the basics of using their device, as well as provide some other helpful tips and tricks. I have done my best to pack great value into this book. Simply put, you're getting more than your money's worth with the information provided in this guide! So let's get started on learning how to get the most out of the iPad Mini for surfing the Internet, using Siri, reading, and other functions.

If this book is helpful, please do not forget to leave a review to let others know!

Apple released the iOS 7 update on September 18, 2013. If you have updated your iPad Mini's operating system, a few of the functions may work slightly differently than those described in this manual. The screens may look different. This guide has been updated with the latest iOS 7 information, and you can check that out in the iOS 7 section of this book.

Table of Contents

Basic Setup

Just like their other products, Apple created the iPad to be incredibly user friendly, and the iPad Mini is an extension of their glorious user-focused design and implementation. However, they do like to keep up with how you use their genius, so you must create an Apple ID to get started with your iPad Mini setup, if you do not already have one.

Create an Apple ID

If you already have an Apple ID that you use for iTunes, iCloud, or the Apple store, you will use the same username and password for your iPad Mini. If you need to create one, click the link that says "I do not have an Apple ID" during setup. Alternatively, you can simply logon to the Apple website from another device to set up an Apple ID before you set up your iPad Mini. Either way, the process is simple. You simply enter a verifiable email address, choose a password, and provide some personal contact information.

After creating your Apple ID, you will receive an email from Apple, asking you to confirm that you are a real person. Once you confirm that you are not a robot, they will guide you through the process of setting up your account. You will be asked to attach a credit card number to the account, which will be charged for any purchases you make through the Apple store, including apps, music, books, and subscriptions.

Connecting to Wi-Fi

Right out of the box, your iPad Mini will ask you to select an available Wi-Fi option after you select your language and country. To connect to Wi-Fi, use the following steps:

1. Type in the name of your current Wi-Fi service.
2. Type in the security code (password) for your current Wi-Fi service.
3. Press "Join."

You can add an additional Wi-Fi network at any time. You would do this if you happen to be enjoying a coffee shop's Wi-Fi, or if you are traveling and need to connect to the hotel's service. Doing this, will not delete the account you use from home or work.

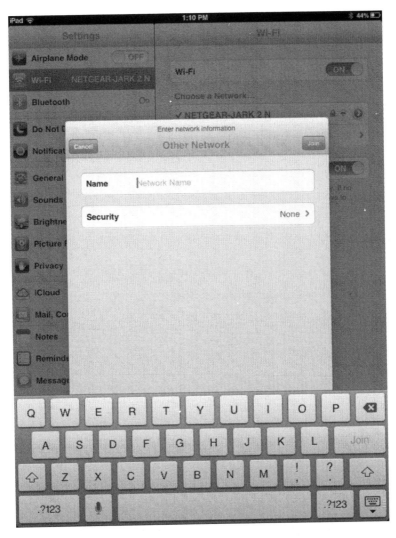

Your iPad Mini will come with 15 preset apps, including staples like the App Store, Calendar, Contacts, and Maps. The most important one of these ever-available selections is the "Settings" app. This app will help you set the time, while providing a quick glimpse at what you your iPad Mini houses. It also allows you to connect to Wi-Fi, using the following steps:

1. Tap the "Settings" App.
2. Tap the "Wi-Fi" option from the side menu.
3. Tap "Add Network" to reveal a pop-up window.
4. Enter the network name.
5. Enter the security code.
6. Tap "Join."

Email Options

There is an email app at the bottom of your iPad Mini that allows you to check your email with a simple tap of the finger. There is no limit to the number of email accounts you can add to your device, which is great for incorporating your work and personal emails into one convenient tablet, so you will always have access on the go.

To add your primary account follow these instructions.

1. Tap the "Settings" app.
2. Locate "Mail, Contacts, Calendars" on the left-hand side of the screen.
3. Enter your name, primary email address (*Helpful Hint:* the one you use as your Apple ID), and your password.

To add a secondary email account simply do the following:

1. Tap the same menu "Mail, Contacts, Calendars."
2. Choose the service your account exists under, such as Google, Yahoo, or AOL.
   NOTE: There is also an option for "other" which will allow you to enter the POP information manually for any account that falls outside of the options listed.

Each email address that is set up on your iPad Mini will deliver email messages to the same inbox, so it will be up to you to keep them separate for work or school if you want to. You can create folders to save different emails into, just as you would on a computer.

How to Open Email Attachment

When you receive an email with an attachment, it will appear as an icon at the end of the email. Simply tap the icon to open the attachment, and view its contents. The iPad Mini will not allow you to download PDF or Word documents to the device. However, pictures can be saved effortlessly after opening them by holding your finger on the actual image until the words "Save Photo" appears as an option. When you do save the image, it will move to the "Photos" app located on the device.

Apple/iTunes Store Log-in

The Apple/iTunes Store provides a bevy of entertainment, and allows you to use your iPad Mini as a multimedia center going forward. You can import your existing iTunes music or buy new music with just a few taps of your finger. You can also purchase books, subscriptions, movies and television shows with just a few swipes of the fingers.

The iTunes icon will be pre-programmed on your iPad Mini, and it is easily recognizable by the musical note emblazoned on the icon. When you tap the icon you will be asked to sign into your account. In order to do so, you simply have to enter the email address that is associated with your Apple ID and the password you set up for that account.

Once you are inside, you are taken to the options Music, Movies, TV Shows, Audiobooks, Top Charts, Genius, and Purchased -- which is a history of everything you have ever bought in the store. You can search these particular categories for new items, and add them to your library. You will be asked again to enter your password before every new purchase, and asked again if you are sure you want to make the purchase, to make sure you do not purchase a song or movie you don't mean to purchase.

Setting up Facebook, Twitter, and Other Social Networks

Setting up your favorite social networks on your iPad Mini is a breeze. You will first have to download the app for each of your preferred social networks, and then set them up with your username and password to have quick access to status updates, tweets, and contact information.

1. Tap the "App Store" icon.
2. Tap and Type "Facebook" (or Twitter, or LinkedIn, etc.) into the search bar at the top, right-hand side of the screen.

3. Locate the App you want to download and tap the word "Free" to reveal the "Install App" button.
4. Tap "Install App" and allow it to download completely before using.
5. Tap the completed app icon for the social network you have downloaded, and enter your username and password for that account.
6. If you do not have an account, follow the prompts within the app to create a profile.

Each time you tap the app icon going forward, it will take you directly inside your account, without having to sign in repeatedly.

Using AirPrint

Your iPad Mini will allow you to print wirelessly to AirPrint enabled printers, as long as they are on the same Wi-Fi network, using the following apps:

- iBooks

- Mail

- Maps

- Notes

- Photos and Camera

- Safari

Depending on which program you are in, tap the printer icon, which is either an arrow facing backwards, or an arrow that appears to be jumping out of a box (it varies depending on the app you are using). Once tapped, the command to print will appear. Tap "Print" and select the printer that is available on your Wi-Fi network. You can also choose the number of copies you would like to print, before giving the final command. Not all printers are AirPrint compatible, but the majority of the popular models like Brother, Hewlett Packard, Epson, and Lexmark are capable of connecting and printing through AirPrint effortlessly. Consult the Apple website for a full list of compatible printers.

Voice to text/SIRI

SIRI is a lovely electronic voice that helps you set appointments or find restaurants and movie reviews. She is the equivalent of a virtual assistant, and she even takes dictation, which is great for composing hand's free emails, text messages, or search topics.

How to activate SIRI

SIRI comes to life when you touch and hold the "Home" button on your iPad Mini. The home button is the indented circle that contains a square icon at the bottom of your iPad Mini. When you hold the button in, you will hear a quick tone, followed by SIRI asking how she can help you.

There are a number of things you can ask SIRI, but if it is not a legitimate question, she will give you a generic answer. For instance, asking her what the meaning of life is, will net you something along the lines of "Traveling a happy and healthy road throughout your existence." However, if you would like to find the closest Chinese restaurant, she is the perfect person to ask.

Sample Questions for SIRI

- Where is the closest Chinese/Italian/Russian/Middle Eastern Restaurant?

- What are the critics saying about (insert movie title here)?

- Where can I find a new rug?

- How many calories are in a banana?

Just be sure to keep your questions short and sweet, while asking them in a clear voice, so she does not mistake your question for something that is not even remotely close. General questions that involve products, services, and locations are all easy for her to answer, and will get you the results you need just by speaking.

How to get SIRI to Type

In order to get SIRI to type, she must be on, and you must be connected to the internet. Begin by displaying the onscreen keyboard and tapping the microphone icon next to the space bar. Begin talking, and allow SIRI to take down everything you say, including the punctuation you would like to use. Tap the microphone icon again to stop the dictation. Tap it again to resume.

If SIRI happens to misunderstand you, and enters the word "Staff" for "Steph," simply change it manually using the keyboard to train her to use the word correctly next time. When you change it during the dictation process, it adds the word to her dictionary, so she can use it properly next time. SIRI is a fast learner, but like most technological assistants, she is not human and cannot comprehend tone or emotion. The best practice is to keep it simple, and annunciate well!

Using FaceTime

FaceTime is Apple's answer to video call programs like Skype. This extremely easy to use application allows you to video chat with anyone who has an Apple device that also has the FaceTime app. The app resembles an older video camera icon, and allows you to make calls to others as long as you are connected to Wi-Fi.

1. Tap the FaceTime icon.
2. Tap Contacts.
3. Choose a Name.
4. Tap the Phone Number or Email Address.

Once you are connected the other person will appear, in real time, on your screen. You will be able to see yourself -- exactly how they see you -- on a smaller screen at the top, corner. You can change the view by tapping the camera icon at the bottom of the screen, which will allow you to show the caller your surroundings, or anything on the other side of the iPad Mini. You can change the view back by tapping the camera icon again.

Using iMessage

Providing yet another way to keep in touch with your contacts, iMessage is a text messaging service on your iPad Mini. The icon is a green square, with a quote bubble. When you tap the icon you will reveal a messaging center that allows you to contact friends through their email address or phone number.

Simply tap the icon that is a square and pencil graphic to create a new message. Begin typing the name of the person you would like to text to reveal a list of contacts similar to your request. You can also tap the "Plus" symbol next to "To:" to display your contacts in alphabetical order. Choose the name once it is revealed, begin typing your text in the space allotted, and press send. You can add more than one person to the conversation by repeating the process until all of the contacts you want to include are listed.

Taking Photos and Videos

The iPad Mini opens up a whole new world for photos and videos by allowing the camera on the back of the device to take in the world around you, or the camera on the front of the device to take self-portraits or video diaries of your day's happenings. Whatever you use the cameras for, you will enjoy the versatility that comes with their programs.

To take pictures, simply tap the Camera app, and the shutter will open to reveal the object(s) within the lens's view. Tap the camera icon on the right-hand side to snap the picture. If you would like to reverse the camera, to take a picture of yourself, simply tap the camera icon on the bottom left that has a rotating arrow around it. You can toggle between the two vantage points as often as you would like. To change the function from camera to video, simply move the slide from the camera icon to the video icon. You will begin recording by tapping the red button on the right-hand side of the screen. Tap it again to stop recording.

How to Edit Photos

After you take the picture, you can view it under the "Photos" app. When you do, tap the picture to reveal a menu across the top. This menu includes the option to "Edit." Tap the edit command to reveal a set of tools at the bottom of the screen including "Rotate," "Enhance," "Remove Red-Eye," and "Crop" as seen in the red box in the photo below.

Simply pick the option you prefer, and make any changes to the picture you want to make. You will be asked to save the edited version once you have finished making changes.

Where to Store Photos and Videos: Cloud vs. Device

You can store the images either on the device or in the cloud. If you launched iCloud when setting up the device, all you have to do to automatically have them saved to the iCloud is tap settings, tap iCloud and turn on "Photo Stream" by tapping the option, and moving the slider into the "On" position. This will allow you to delete them from the device, but maintain them in the cloud, to avoid using the available memory on the iPad Mini for image storage.

Sharing Photos and Videos to Social Networks

If you are a huge fan of sharing your experiences on your social networks, it could not be easier than it is with the iPad Mini. Select the picture from your photo gallery and tap it once to reveal the media options menu at the top. This is the same place you found the "Edit" option before. This will reveal an icon of a forward arrow that appears to be exiting a box. Tap the icon to reveal a number of sharing options including:

- Mail.

- Message.

- Photo Stream.

- Any Social Networks you have on the Device (Facebook, Twitter, Pinterest, etc.).

- Assign to Contacts.

Tap the icon on which you would like to share the photo. It will immediately assemble a window, where you can add text if you choose before posting it in its entirety.

How to Delete Pictures

When you want to delete a picture, simply tap the image to reveal the menu bar at the top of the image. The last icon, on the upper, right-hand side of the page is a trash can. Tap the icon, and you will be prompted with the command "Delete Photo." Tap it to dispose of the image.

Playing Music

There are several options for playing Music on your iPad Mini. This section covers several options including iTunes, Amazon Cloud Player, Spotify, and Pandora.

Syncing iPad Mini to iTunes

Because it is an iPad Mini, iTunes automatically comes loaded on the device. This is great if you already have an iPod or use the program on your computer because you can sync this device to your existing iTunes library. There are two methods to obtaining your existing music through your new iPad Mini. First, you can tap the iTunes icon and locate the tab "Purchased" at the bottom. It will provide the option to sync any purchases made on another device to this one. Next, in order to sync your complete iTunes account to your iPad Mini, you must plug your device into your computer or laptop where the source of your iTunes account lies. Use the accompanying USB cable, and plug it into the computer. Open iTunes on the computer, and allow it to recognize the iPad Mini. Once it does, sync the two devices by clicking "Sync" in the iTunes menu. Your iTunes will be updated, and ready to use at any time.

Amazon Cloud Player App (Free)

Because not everything you have purchased to date came from the iTunes Store, you may need to download an additional app to gain access to the rest of your media. The Amazon Cloud Player App is free, and it gives you complete access to any music, movies, books, or television shows you purchased through Amazon. Tap the App Store icon, and search for the app by name.

Spotify (Free or Premium)

Spotify is an online music source that gives users access to millions of songs, through a free subscription, that gives you unlimited listening for the first six months, with radio-style advertising. You must have a Facebook account to join Spotify, and if you do not update your account to the Premium option, your listening will be limited to ten hours per month after the initial six month period, broken into 2.5 hour increments. Tap the App Store icon, and search for the app by name.

Pandora

Pandora is a lot like Spotify in that it is brought to you for free, thanks to its sponsors. This means there are commercials in between songs, just like a regular radio station. The difference is, Pandora allows you to personalize your listening, so you can dictate the music you hear. For instance, if you enter "Nirvana," it will play an assembly of grunge, including the band you chose, and bands like them. Tap the App Store icon, and search for the app by name.

Watching Videos/Movies

There are a number of ways to watch your favorite videos, television shows, and movies on your iPad Mini. Depending on your viewing preferences, you may need to download apps that carry your current or desired subscriptions, so you are only a tap away from all of your favorites.

YouTube is a popular video sanctuary that allows users to view anything and everything that other users upload. It can be movies, commercials, music videos, or even stunts that go terribly, terribly wrong. YouTube is available through a free app via the App Store, or can be accessed through the Safari web browser at YouTube.com.

Amazon Instant Video

If you are an Amazon Prime member, Amazon Instant Video gives you free access to over 140,000 videos. What's more is a user can download movies to the device, so you can view them without a Wi-Fi connection. This is perfect for traveling on planes, trains, or cars. Tap the App Store icon, and search for the app by name.

Netflix

Netflix is a subscription service that allows its members to view unlimited movies and television shows for a monthly fee. The app delivers their entire library into the palm of your hands, if you have an account. Tap the App Store icon, and search for the app by name.

Hulu-Plus

Hulu-Plus is also available by subscription, and allows members to view all of their favorite television shows as they are happening. You do not have to wait until the season is over, you simply have to log in and choose the ones you missed, sit back and enjoy the show. Tap the App Store icon, and search for the app by name.

How to Read Kindle eBooks (app)

The Kindle app for iPad is a perfect way to enjoy all of your favorite eBooks, magazines, newspapers and even textbooks using your iPad Mini, instead of an actual Kindle. This free app also gives you access to the Kindle store, allowing you purchase new books or subscriptions at any time. The interface gives the illusion of using a Kindle, saving the last page read, and allowing you to highlight passages, make notes and bookmark sections. Tap the App Store icon, and search for the app by name.

How to Read Other eBooks

If you are enjoying free eBooks from all around the web, it is possible to sync those selections onto your iPad Mini, and enjoy them through the iBooks app. From your computer, open your iTunes program. Drag the downloaded eBook file to the "Books" segment of the iTunes library and allow it to transfer completely. Sync your iPad Mini with your computer, and you can read the eBook through the iBooks source.

Using the Web

Your iPad Mini comes equipped with the Safari browser. To use it effectively, this section provides a few tips to guide you around the World Wide Web.

Adding Bookmarks

There are a number of reasons for bookmarking a web page. The first is usually because you frequent the sites including your bank or daily news, and would prefer to get to each with a single tap. To do so, tap the forward arrow escaping a box icon, and choose "Bookmark" from the available options. You can see an example of this inside the red box in the screen-shot below.

To get to the bookmarks later, tap the open book icon to view the saved sites.

Pin Websites to Home Screen

When you would like to add a website to your home screen, so you have even quicker access to it without going through Safari, tap the forward arrow escaping a box icon, and choose "Add to Home Screen" from the available options. This will create an icon on your home screen for that particular website.

Change Default Search Engine

The iPad Mini's default search engine is Google, but it can be changed for those who prefer Bing or Yahoo.

1. Tap the "Settings" Icon.
2. Tap "Safari" from Menu on the left-hand side.
3. Tap "Search Engine" at the top of the page.
4. Choose from Google, Bing, or Yahoo.

You can change your iPad Mini's default search engine as often as you would like.

Private Browsing

Private browsing allows you to protect your private information by limiting websites from tracking your online behavior. In order to enjoy private browsing, you must turn it on first. You can also turn it off at any time going forward.

1. Tap "Settings" Icon.

2. Tap "Safari" from Menu on the left-hand side.
3. Locate "Private Browsing" under the "Privacy" section.
4. Move the Slider to "On."

Other Browsers

There are a number of other browsers that are available for the iPad Mini, but not all of them are free, and they are not necessarily adding to the browsing experience any more than Safari does. However, since not everyone is a fan of Safari, they may be worth researching to receive a truly personal online experience. Each is available in the App Store, and can be located by a search of their names.

- Chrome: Free

- Atomic Browser: $.99

- iCabMobile: $1.99

- Perfect Browser: $1.99

- Skyfire: $4.99

Miscellaneous Web Options

There are a number of things web surfers become accustomed to doing on their computers, and when you first start using an iPad Mini the commands may seem foreign. Never fear: You can copy, paste and take screen shots just like you can with your trusty laptop.

How to Download an Image from the Web to iPad Photos

When you see a picture you just have to have, whether it is on a social media site, or your favorite news outlet, all you have to do is place your finger directly on the image and hold it there until the command "Save Image" appears. Tap save image, and the picture will automatically be stored in your Photos.

How to Copy and Paste

When you would like to highlight a passage to pass along to a friend in an email, or to post elsewhere, simply place your finger over the text until it is highlighted. The words "Copy" and "Define" will show up. You can see an example of this in the screen-shot below. Use the blue buttons that appear to increase or decrease the area or text you would like to copy, and then tap "Copy." Place your finger on the screen where you are pasting the information and hold it until the words "Paste" appears. Tap "Paste," and the text you just copied will appear.

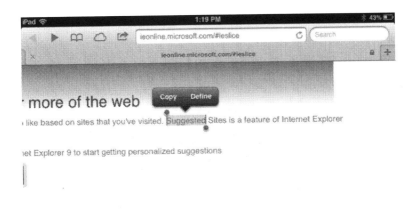

more of the web

Copy Define

like based on sites that you've visited. Suggested Sites is a feature of Internet Explorer

et Explorer 9 to start getting personalized suggestions

rs also liked:

🟥 MySpace	cนn CNN.com - Break...	🔲 Windows Live
rch the Web, Features ac...	An international site that offers email, a forum, communities, videos and weblog space.	CNN.com delivers the latest breaking news and information on the latest top stories, w...	Keep in touch with family and through e-mail, instant messa unified cont...

I Listen to Free Music Online - Free Music Streaming ... visitors also liked:

Radio - ...	🔴 Yahoo! Music - I...	⚪ Grooveshark - Lis...	▶ Free Music Vic
personalized that helps you	Find music videos, internet radio, music downloads and all the latest music news and ...	Listen to any song in the world for free. Create free internet radio stations. Search fo...	Watch free music videos, tun AOL Radio, get free music downloads, read musi...

acy | Trademarks | © 2013 Microsoft

How to Take a Screen Shot

When you want to capture a story, headline, or comment that may disappear later, you can take a screen shot of exactly what you see, the moment you see it. Simply press and hold the home button, and the sleep button at the top of the iPad Mini at the same time. The screenshot will appear in your photos.

How to set up Form AutoFill Option

If you find yourself filling out a lot of online forms, form auto-fill may be a valuable, time-saving tool for you. When active, this option will automatically add your general information to online forms, including your name, address, email address, and phone number. To activate the auto-fill function:

1. Tap "Settings."
2. Tap "Safari" from the left-hand side menu.
3. Select "AutoFill" from the list.
4. Move the Slider to "On" to use your Contact Information to AutoFill Forms.

iPad Mini How Tos

The iPad Mini is a really great tool for work or play, and can be personalized to help you optimize your time using the power of organization.

How to use iPad Shortcuts

When you would like to add shortcuts to your system, to expedite your entries, all you have to do it program them into your iPad Mini.

1. Tap "Settings."
2. Tap "General" from the left-hand side menu.
3. Tap "Keyboard" from the bottom of the list.
4. Tap "Add New Shortcut" from the bottom of the list.
5. Add the word or phrase that you want to create a shortcut for in the allotted space.

How to Create App Folders

If you would like to organize your apps into folders, so all of your games or subscriptions are in one place, all you have to do is create the folder and name it.

To Create a Folder:

1. Place and hold your finger on an app, until it begins to jiggle.

2. Drag the app to another app you would like it to appear with, and drop it on top of it.

The folder will appear, allowing you to add as many apps as you would like to it.

To change the Name of the Folder:

1. Tap the folder to open it.
2. Tap the name.
3. Type in a different one.

To remove an App from a Folder:

1. Select the App you want to remove.
2. Drag the app outside of the folder.

To delete a Folder

Simply drag all of the apps outside of the folder, and it will disappear.

How to Dock Apps

When you would like to "Dock" an app to the bottom of the screen, so it is always visible, simply place your finger on the app until it begins to jiggle. Move the app by dragging it with your finger to the bottom of the screen until it appears in the lineup where you want it. Hit the home screen button at the bottom of the iPad Mini to set the new placement.

How to Make Your Own Wallpaper

When you want to personalize your iPad Mini by making your own wallpaper, instead of having the standard issue background that comes with the device, follow these quick steps.

1. Tap "Settings."
2. Tap "Brightness & Wallpaper" from the left-hand side menu.
3. Tap the "Wallpaper" graphic.
4. Choose "Camera Roll" and pick your own image to appear as wallpaper.

How to Turn Off Keyboard Clicks

If the constant clicking sound that accompanies your typing becomes a bother, you can turn it off with just a few steps.

1. Tap "Settings."
2. Tap "Sounds" from the left-hand side menu.
3. Move the "Keyboard Clicks" slider to "Off."

How to Multitask

When you would like to multitask, or bounce back and forth between apps, simply push the home button at the bottom of your device twice. This will allow you to stay on your email screen while displaying the other available apps at the bottom of the screen. Tap another app to go directly to it, or slide the apps from left to right to display more app options.

How to Use the Notifications Bar

The side of your iPad Mini device has two functions. One is the volume, which can be turned up or down simply by pressing it in either direction. The second function is a notification bar, which can be enabled by sliding it to reveal a bell with a line through it on the screen. This will completely silence any notifications that you may receive while it is enabled.

How to Extend Battery Life

If you are watching a movie, there really is no way to keep the battery level from decreasing along the way. However, if you are not actively using the iPad Mini, there are a number of ways to extend the battery life. You do not have to use all of them at once, but any combination will help.

- Keep Your Software Updated: This will help all programs, apps, and operating systems running optimally, causes less battery lag.
- Adjust the Brightness: Using less light means using less battery. Tap "Settings" and "Brightness & Wallpaper" to adjust the slider for a minimal brightness level that still allows you to see clearly.
- Lock the Device: When you are not using your iPad Mini, tap the sleep/wake button on the top to lock the device. This will dim the screen immediately, while using very little energy.
- Turn off "Push" Notices: When you download an app, or sign up for a service, you will be asked to receive "Push Notifications." This basically means the app wants to update you throughout the day on whatever it is that is happening. For instance, news sites push breaking news, and social media sites push comments and status updates. This causes your iPad Mini to light up more often, which causes a significant drain on the battery.

How to use Parental Controls

Keeping your little ones from accessing mature material, making unauthorized purchases, or simply logging into your email and sending a weird message to your newest client is a simple process. Once the restrictions are enabled, you will need to enter your passcode to access the protected app(s) going forward.

1. Tap "Settings."
2. Locate and tap "Restrictions" from the menu.
3. Tap "Enable Restrictions."
4. Move the slider to enable/disable the restrictions on each available option as you see fit.

How to Download Google Maps

Apple has decided to operate their own mapping systems in their devices, instead of using Google as they have in the past. The problem is, their maps are not very accurate or user friendly. Although their technology continues to improve from its first iteration, Google Maps is still the go-to mapping software for the masses.

To download the latest version, simply tap the App Store icon, and search for the Google Maps by name. It is a free download, and will help you maneuver the world a lot easier, whether it is on foot, bicycle, or by car.

How to Delete Apps

Deleting an app from your iPad Mini only takes a couple of seconds. Locate the app you would like to delete and place your finger directly on its icon until it begins to jiggle. When it does, an "x" will appear on the upper, left-hand corner of the icon. Press the "x" to remove the app from your device. You will be asked if you are "Sure you want to delete (name of app)?" Tap yes to delete it completely.

How to Delete Files

Deleting files is as simple as deleting apps. Simply locate the file in your iTunes library or in your iCloud, highlight it and hit delete. You will be asked again if you want to delete the file, before it disappears for good.

How to Print from iPad

If you do not have a WIFI enabled printer to use AirPrint, or do not own one of the compatible versions listed on the Apple website, printing may still be possible with the addition of an app. Research your printer online, and determine if there is an app that is downloadable to allow you to print from your iPad to the printer. Each printer is different, and although companies are trying to keep up with wireless technology, they all have not gotten there yet.

If you are able to print wirelessly, simply tap the forward arrow escaping a box icon, and hit "Print" to test your new app.

How to use AirPlay with Apple TV

Apple TV has opened the iPad user to a whole new world of device interaction. An Apple TV is a small box that plugs directly into your television or cable receiver. When you have an Apple TV device, your iPad Mini will recognize it wirelessly, and allow you to play movies, videos, music, and photos directly on the television through AirPlay. The television becomes a mirror of what is happening on the iPad, and you can make that happen in just a few steps.

While you are inside of an app, whether it is iTunes or YouTube, simply tap the icon at the top of the page that resembles as flat screen television sitting on a black triangle. Once pressed, the option of "Apple TV" will appear. Tap the option, and watch your television screen to see the same thing you are seeing on your iPad Mini. You can remove the images from the screen by tapping the option again, to return to your regularly scheduled programming.

How to use VoiceOver

VoiceOver is an option on the iPad Mini that allows you to hear what is happening on screen, without seeing it. When this option is enabled, you must perform gestures to control the iPad Mini. When they do, it delivers the text on screen, images or information as it reads from the left hand corner first. The user can prompt VoiceOver to engage in the information that is on the screen by asking it to "double tap" the passage to hear more.

Once the VoiceOver option is engaged, it requires gestures to operate the iPad Mini going forward; even to turn the option off again.

To enable VoiceOver:

1. Tap "Settings."
2. Tap "General."
3. Tap "Accessibility."
4. Tap "VoiceOver."

As you drag your finger over the screen, VoiceOver describes each item you touch.

How to use Do Not Disturb

The Do Not Disturb option on your iPad Mini keeps any notifications from sounding or lighting up the screen. You can still use the alarm function while in Do Not Disturb mode, however, which is perfect for traveling. To set the device to Do Not Disturb mode:

1. Tap "Settings."
2. Tap "Notifications."
3. Set "Do Not Disturb."

You can personalize who or what gets through to you, so if you are okay with receiving FaceTime calls from a certain person, or to schedule blocks of quiet time, you can program the function to recognize those commands.

iPad Trouble Shooting

If there is one thing that is certain in the technological world, it is that devices are not always running optimally. A glitch here, a malfunctioning app there, and a complete freeze from time to time are the price you pay for enjoying any electronic device. Although Apple prides itself on its superior user satisfaction, there can be times when you simply need to reset your iPad Mini to shake the cobwebs from its functionality. There are also times when you are going to need to locate the device after inadvertently misplacing it. Luckily, Apple has thought of just about everything. Now, if it could only go to work for you.

How to Reset the iPad Mini

Usually, restarting the iPad Mini -- by turning it off and back on -- will fix any issue you are having, including a frozen screen or application. If that does not work, and only when that does not work, it may be necessary to reset your iPad Mini.

To reset the device complete the following steps:

1. Hold the "Sleep/Wake" button and the "Home" button at the same time, for at least ten seconds.
2. The Apple logo appears, signifying the device has been fully reset.
3. Simply proceed where you left off, once the iPad Mini reboots completely.

How to Find Your iPad Mini

There is a free app available called "Find iPhone (iPad or iPod -- any will work)" that can be downloaded to your iPad Mini to help you locate it in a moment of panic. Once it has been downloaded it will walk you through the process of setting up iCloud (if you have not already) to turn the feature on. This feature allows you to locate your iPad Mini by signaling it to release a loud, continuous sound for up to two minutes while you locate the device around your home, in your car, or anywhere else that you may have been recently. If it is somewhere you are not, the sound is definitely going to get someone's attention, so you may want to warn them via a text message from your phone, or email from your computer first.

If someone has stolen the device, you can access the feature to wipe the iPad Mini clean of your personal information and any media on the device, restoring it to its factory settings. This is the worst case scenario, but is certainly an option if you feel like the device's contents could cause personal damage in the wrong hands. That is to say that if you have personal information regarding financials or relationships that you would rather not go viral, wiping it clean may be your best bet. If you have enabled your iCloud account, you have nothing to worry about. You can get it all back in an instant.

If you have lost the device, and are certain that a nice person is willing to return it, you can send a message to the iPad Mini, locking it from use, while displaying only your contact information so the finder can locate you to return it. This feature also allows you to track the device's whereabouts, so you can begin the hunt to get it back quickly.

From your device, after you have downloaded the free app, follow these steps to turn on the feature:

1. Tap "Settings."
2. Tap "iCloud."
3. Move the Slider to the App's Description to "On."

How to Clean the iPad Mini Screen

When you need to clean your iPad Mini screen, be sure to disconnect it from any cords or peripherals, and turn the device off. Use a soft, lint-free cloth to wipe the device clean. Do not use household cleaning agents or compressed air to clean the screen, as both can cause damage to the device's composition. You should also avoid getting any liquid into any of the openings at all times.

iPad Mini Apps

With millions of apps clamoring for downloads, the App Store is a virtual hotspot for all things entertainment. In addition, there are a number of corporate and professional apps available that provide function and ease to your daily life, at the ready by simply tapping the icon.

If you know the name of the app you are looking for, say something along the lines of "Bank of America" or "The Weather Channel" simply tap the App Store icon on your screen, and enter the name into the search bar at the top. Chances are you will receive more than one option as a result. However, some have the proper name of the establishment you are looking for, and can be verified by tapping the app to reveal more information before you download it.

You can also search for apps based on keywords such as "Diet Tracker" or "Nutritional Information" if you would like to find an app that allows you to journal your food and exercise habits. No matter what you are looking for, there is an app for it, and it can be found with a simple keyword search, much like an Internet search. Just think in the same terms, and you will be whisked away to an endless supply of options in no time.

Free vs. Paid (Premium Versions) Apps

When you do begin searching and reviewing apps you will notice that some are free, and some are premium versions that you have to pay for. Free apps almost always come with advertisements, unless they are from a professional affiliation like your bank or PayPal. When you pay for a premium service, you are usually paying to be void of advertisements in print, video, or sound.

The application does not usually differ from the free to paid version, although some will supply an additional service when you are using the paid version. Be sure to read the reviews of each app before you download it. Users provide some of the best insight into what works and what does not.

Examples of Good Free Apps

Downloading fun and functional apps can help turn your iPad Mini into a resource of information, while allowing it to serve as a multi-media platform. These free apps will help you maneuver through everyday life, while having a little fun along the way.

Alarm Clock App: Perfect for traveling, or simply using a different device besides your cellphone, which can become interruptive to your sleeping habits.

Weather App: The best part of having a weather app on your iPad Mini is that it will change its updates depending on your location, giving you the day's weather report for whichever city you are in. It also allows you to look ahead at what's to come in any city you would like to add by entering the zip code of your choice.

Television Apps: NBC and ABC both have an app that allows you to watch episodes from their network's shows with just a couple of taps of the fingers. This is perfect for catching up with your favorite sitcom, or watching soap operas.

News Outlet Apps: Not all news outlets require a subscription to enjoy the daily headlines, which means you can view all of the day's news in easy to access blocks of information. CNN is free, and allows you to choose your edition to encompass your interests.

Stocks Apps: Keeping an eye on the pulse of Wall Street has never been easier with the menagerie of stock apps available for the iPad Mini. In fact, there are a number of designs and layouts that allow you to pick the stream you enjoy personally.

Sports Apps: If you would like to view the latest scores and headlines or simply follow your favorite sport individually, there is an app to provide maximum coverage of everything from football to soccer. The ESPN app allows you pick your favorite teams, and save them so that you are alerted to their upcoming game times, scores and highlights, while enjoying the rest of the sporting world at the same time. If you would like to pick and choose your sports, MLB, NFL, and NBA all have apps that reflect the insight of their organizations each day, including scores, highlights, and player information.

Banking Apps: If you enjoy online banking from your computer, be sure to download the banking app for your account to your iPad Mini. It will allow you quick and easy access to balances, charges, statements, and may even allow you to deposit your check virtually. All banks are different, so check the capabilities of yours specifically when you search for it in the App Store.

Informative & Curiosity Driven Apps: There are going to be thousands of times when you reach for your iPad Mini to get help answering a question, or identifying the actress in a movie you are watching. A couple of the best apps to keep on hand for these types of inquiries is the IMDb app, which will give you all of the information you could ever want about movies, television shows, casts, credits, and reviews the moment you tap its icon. In addition, the Wikipedia app can provide you with a quick search option to find out the history behind the scar on your favorite actor or writer's forehead. Lastly, the Dictionary.com app is perfect for delivering definitions to your screen in a matter of seconds.

Calculator: Turn your iPad Mini into a calculator by downloading your favorite style in an app. Whether you are an engineer, scientist, or someone who just wants to add up their grocery expenditures, there is a calculator that will suit your needs.

Games: You absolutely cannot go wrong with Angry Birds. It allows you to plan a strategy of launching birds into structures to score points, while enjoying the vivid graphics and fun sounds the game delivers. If you are interested in word games or matching games and racing games or shooting games, all you have to do is search the App Store with any of the keywords that come to mind when you think of your interests. The store will deliver a number of results for you to choose from, so you can never go wrong. You also might bump into something you never knew existed, and enjoy it even more!

iPad Mini Accessories

There are a number of iPad Mini accessories on the market that will help maximize the life of your device, while delivering versatile usability going forward. Check out even more details at Techmediasource.

Screen Protector

Your iPad Mini screen will come with fingerprint-resistant oleophobic (oil repellant) coating, but it does not last forever. Instead of allowing it to wear with time, protect your screen from the beginning with a clear screen protector that keeps fingerprints to a minimum, while helping to avoid scratching, nicking or overall wear on the device. The protector is a clear adhesive material -- typically sold in threes -- that applies directly to the screen, delivering a protective layer. You will notice a huge difference in the lack of smudging, and the overall glare on the screen when you apply a protector.

Cases

Cases serve more than one purpose when you place your device inside of one. First, it delivers a protective approach the iPad Mini's use. Second, it allows you to personalize your iPad Mini by purchasing different designs and styles. The first attribute is the most important, of course, as it helps you protect your Mini from any drops, spills, or scratching during transit. It also keeps it safe from the elements, should you get caught in the wind, rain, or snow with your device in tow. There are hard cases, leather cases, cloth cases, and even different styles that allow you to simply cover the back, the front, or the whole device. Obviously these cases are available in a huge variety of colors and prints to compliment your personal style.

Stands

Stands may not be the first thing you think of when you purchase an iPad Mini, but they certainly come in handy for a number of reasons. If your use your device in the kitchen to help prepare meals or to look up a recipe, a stand is perfect for keeping the device out of harm's way. You certainly do not want flour, grease, or liquids to make their way onto the device in any form, and a stand will help lift it for protection. In addition, if you use the device in a store, as way to checkout or display information, a stand will keep in stationary for others to use. A stand might also be helpful during FaceTime conversations if you do not want to hold your iPad for long talks. They can also be used for presentations, or to hold the device in place while you type on a Bluetooth keyboard.

Bluetooth Keyboard

If you use your iPad Mini for more than just movies and banking, you may find that the onscreen keyboard has its limits. If so, a Bluetooth keyboard is perfect for you. The wireless keyboard works just like a regular computer keyboard, and allows you to type on your iPad Mini quickly and efficiently. In fact, some even provide a stand for your iPad Mini, allowing it to resemble an actual laptop when it is connected. The picture below shows a case with a Bluetooth keyboard.

Stylus

If you do not want to use your fingers to type or turn the page of your book, there is a stylus pen that will help you maneuver around your iPad Mini without leaving any fingerprints. In addition, the rubber-tipped pen allows you to draw, make notes on documents, or provide interesting graphics to a presentation.

Cables/Adaptors (HDMI, VGA, USB, etc.)

Since the iPad Mini operates as a wireless device, typically the last thing on anyone's mind is purchasing actual wires to increase its versatility. There are a number of cables and adaptors that will turn your iPad Mini into a true multi-media device, starting with the USB cable. The USB cable allows you to sync your iPad to your computer, while transferring information seamlessly between the two.

The HDMI cable allows you to transfer media from the iPad Mini to another source in high definition for home entertainment networking. It allows you to link your iPad Mini to a television or media screen to view the onscreen items on a larger format. Movies, pictures, and videos can all be transferred flawlessly with the use of an HDMI cable.

The VGA, or Video Graphics Array, cable allows you to transfer video. Usually a cable that connects a computer to a monitor, the cable has expanded its value and allows the iPad Mini to be used on HD televisions, media centers, and projectors of more advanced systems.

The Car Charger: As technology evolves, one thing remains constant -- the car charger. This easy to tote and use device allows your iPad Mini to stay charged on the go, which is perfect for traveling, sales calls, and field work.

Additional Accessories for Individual Users

There is a range of accessories available that will help turn your iPad Mini into a completely different device as needed. Everyone from new mommies to musicians use their iPad Minis for different reasons, and Apple has listened to each need individually, and tried to fill it.

The Microphone: There is a microphone accessory available for the iPad Mini, which is great for everything from speeches to concerts. You simply insert the microphone to the proper outlet on the device, and you can record minutes from a meeting effortlessly. What's more is that there is also a microphone stand accessory for the iPad Mini, which will allow you to use the device as a teleprompter, if you so desire.

Wireless Speakers: Since you already have your music library on your device, why not play it for others to enjoy? There are a number of wireless speaker brands and varieties that will allow you to stream music from your iPad Mini wirelessly through your Bluetooth option, which is perfect for parties and cookouts or even just listing to your playlists while cleaning your house.

Camera/Surveillance Technology: It is possible to keep an eye on your home, office, or kids while you are away by using the Bluetooth technology that is available on your iPad Mini. Compatible cameras are available in small, undetectable sizes and can be set up anywhere and watching from a remote location through your device. This is the perfect way to turn your device into a baby monitor, or to keep an eye on aging parents.

The Camera Connection Kit: Perfect for plugging into your iPad Mini, the camera connection kit allow users to transfer information, videos, or images from their cameras SD cards to the iPad Mini effortlessly. In addition, it allows you to plug your camera directly into the kit through a USB cord.

iOS 7 Update

Apple released the iOS 7 update on September 18, 2013. The following sections detail the changes that the new iOS 7 Update made to the iPhone 5.

The iOS 7 update could take around 20 to 30 minutes or longer depending on your connection speed and other factors. First, the new software will download to your device. Once it has, you'll be asked to tap on another option and the update will begin "Verifying" for several moments. Once verified, your device will automatically shut off to a black screen, and the Apple logo will appear in the center of your screen. A progress bar will show underneath as the update officially installs.

Once your update has installed, you'll be able to get going with the new iOS 7 upgrade. You'll be asked to select your wireless connection, enable location services (if you choose), and you'll be asked to sign in to your iCloud account (if you choose) to activate certain aspects of the update.

Standard Apps Updated

In iOS 7, Apple has made updates to some of their basic apps mentioned in this guide. They include the Notes, Photos, Weather and Camera app. They all have newly-designed interfaces, and in a few cases some new features added in. For example, the camera feature now allows for organizing your photos in different ways than before.

The Safari web browser now features a slicker interface complete with the ability to use the address bar as a search bar.

Also, Apple has made it an option that device users can have all of their apps "auto-update" when needed. This will get rid of that red notification number you see on your Apps icon on the screen, as the apps will update without needing you to do so manually. Keep in mind, setting your apps to "auto-update" could update some apps to new versions with bugs that you might want to think twice about before using.

SIRI iOS 7 Change

In iOS 7, the helpful SIRI voice assistant is still present, but now has a new interface, and new voices to use.

Search iOS 7 Change

In the previous version of the iOS, search was accessed simply by swiping to the left of your main screen on your device. Now, to access search, you'll need to swipe down from the center of your home screen to access the search field.

The Control Center

You can access the new Control Center from any screen you're on. Simply swipe your finger up from the very bottom edge of the screen and it will reveal the Control Center bar across the bottom of your display. Let's go through what you'll see there.

At the left side of your Control Center, you'll see controls for music. If you are currently playing music on your device, you'll be able to lower or raise the volume, play or pause the song, as well as move forward or backwards to the next song, or previous song, respectively.

In the center of your Control Center you should see five circles with different icons in them. These allow you to quickly enable or disable the following:

- Airplane mode: for when you are traveling by plane and need to shut off wireless access.
- Wireless: to enable or disable your Wi-Fi connection
- Bluetooth: to enable or disable your Bluetooth for your device.
- Do Not Disturb: to enable or disable settings you have on your device which prevent sounds or other notifications. This may be helpful during meetings, at

the movies, or if you have the device near you while sleeping.

- Portrait Orientation Lock: To lock your device so it only displays in portrait view (vertically). When this is locked and you turn your device sideways it will not switch to the landscape display.

Underneath the five icons are AirDrop and AirPlay.

- AirDrop was added as a feature on iOS 7. By tapping on Airdrop, you can enable whether the feature is On or Off. Additionally you can choose to be "discoverable" by only the people you have listed on your device's contacts, or you can set it so that everyone can discover your device to share files. Remember, Airdrop will only work between Apple devices that have this feature enabled.
- AirPlay is for using your iPad Mini to transmit a mirror image of what's displaying on your iPad Mini an Apple TV (if you have one, and it has AirPlay enabled).

Finally on the right side of your Control Center are two more icons and another adjustment bar.

- Clock/Timer - tap on this second icon to quickly access the timer and clock functions on your device.
- Camera - tap on the fourth and final icon to quickly access your device's camera.

Below these two icons, you'll see a bar to adjust your screen display brightness. Slide towards the left to dim the display, or towards the right to brighten your display.

There are a few settings you can change for your Control Center, if you choose to. Here's how to:

Go to Settings > Control Center

- You can switch the "Access on Lock Screen" On or Off.
- You can switch the "Access Within Apps" On or Off.

The first setting will be helpful if you want to be able to access your Control Center easily when your device is locked. If this is enabled you won't have to enter a pass code in order to get to Control Center.

The second setting might be helpful if you want to avoid inadvertently swiping your Control Center onto the screen while playing a game, for example.

iTunes Radio

Another new feature within iOS 7 is the iTunes Radio. This feature is very similar to Pandora's online streaming music service, for those familiar with it. iTunes doesn't charge for use of their radio, but you'll need to have Wi-Fi or other access to stream the music to your device.

To access the Radio, tap on the "Music" app icon on your device home screen (usually among the bottom four app icons on your display). The Radio icon will be the first one in the bottom left corner of your iTunes display. Tap on it to enable iTunes Radio.

Once there, you'll be presented with "Featured Stations" you can scroll through at the very top. You can simply tap on any of those and it will start playing music from those particular radio stations, based on your musical tastes. Or, you can also tap on the "Edit" word you see on iTunes radio, which will allow you to add to your list of "My Stations." This will provide you quicker access to your favorite stations for listening on the go.

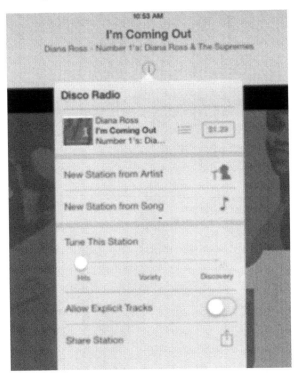

When you're playing a song and it is displaying on your screen, you'll also have options at the top of your screen, including an "i" in a red circle. This brings up more listening options including the ability to generate a new station, as well as the option to "allow explicit tracks" or share the station with others. You'll also have the option on this screen to purchase the current song from iTunes Music Store.

Note: *Remember, through the Control Center (swiping up from the bottom of any screen), you can increase/decrease music volume, pause the song, or even click on the "star." That star will bring up the options to "Play More Like This," "Never Play This Song" or Add to iTunes Wish List."*

Multitasking Abilities

Apple added in the ability for more convenient multitasking with the iOS 7 update. This newly-improved layout allows you to easily move between open apps and close the ones you no longer want to use. By double-tapping on your home button, you can view all of your open apps on one screen. The display is now improved, and each app appears as a small card image. To close out of an open app, simply swipe the card upward.

Airdrop Feature

A brand new featured unveiled in iOS 7 is called Airdrop. This feature allows users to share photos or other files with nearby iPhone or Mac users (if their device supports Airdrop).

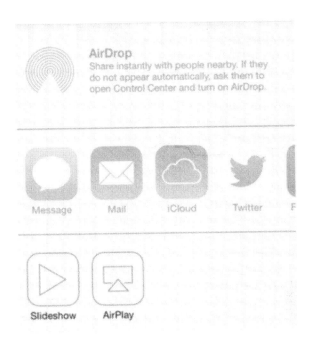

To use the feature, you'll be using the area Wi-Fi or a Bluetooth connection to drag a photo to another person's device that has Airdrop. It will work between iPhones and iPads that have iOS 7 with AirDrop enabled, and as of this publication, it was said to work with various Apple computers that have AirDrop.

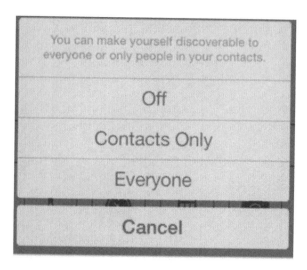

You can make yourself discoverable to everyone or only people in your contacts.

Off

Contacts Only

Everyone

Cancel

How to Enable AirDrop Feature:

- Swipe up from the bottom of your device to bring up Control Center.
- Tap on Airdrop.
- You'll get a menu that comes up with "Off," "Contacts Only" and "Everyone." Select one of the latter two options and tap on it to enable AirDrop, depending on who you want to share files with.

Once AirDrop is enabled, you'll be able to share photos with those nearby who have AirDrop activated. You can share photos straight from your camera roll or right after you take a photo or video.

How to Share a Photo With AirDrop

- After taking a photo tap on that photo, (or go to your Photos or Camera icon on the main screen to access your camera photo roll).
- Next go to the small share icon in the left bottom corner of the screen on the photo you want to share. Tap on

that icon to bring up options for sharing, including "AirDrop."

- Anyone in the vicinity who has AirDrop enabled should show up as an option in a small circle icon. You can tap on that person's name/circle to share the photo with. (Note: You may need to wait a few moments for contracts to show up on your photo share as Airdrop discovers who is nearby.)
- Once you've shared it, the person should receive a pop-up box on their device as seen below, where they can Decline or Accept the photo.

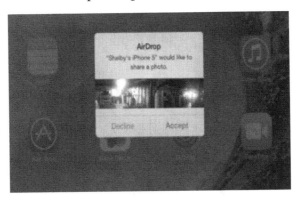

Remember, you can easily turn "AirDrop" on or off by swiping up from the bottom of any screen and tapping "AirDrop" on your Control Center, then selecting the appropriate option.

Note: *Keep in mind this feature may not work with all file types and in all apps on your device, and as mentioned will only work with Airdrop-supported devices.*

New Camera Features

The camera app on your device was upgraded during the iOS 7 update. It now has a slick new interface display. When you first access the camera, you'll start off in regular photo mode. However, when you swipe your down the screen, you'll now be in Video mode. If you swipe your finger up on the photo screen, you'll get to Square mode.

Square mode allows you to take a perfectly square image with its dimensions the same for side-to-side and up-to-down of the photo.

In addition to the modes, once you go to your latest photo taken, or your photo roll, you can tap on "Edit" up in the right hand corner of your display. This will bring up a host of options you can use to edit your photo including Rotate, Enhance, Filters, Red Eye and Crop.

Remember that once you take a photo, you can simply go to your "Photos" icon on your device's main screen, tap on it, and find the latest photos you've taken. You can then share these in different ways including via text message, email, Facebook, Twitter, or print them.